AF351315

River of Life

Poetry and Photography

Renée Ametane'e Roman Nose,

Cheyenne and Arapaho Tribes of Oklahoma

River of Life

Poetry and Photography

Renée Ametane'e Roman Nose,
Cheyenne and Arapaho Tribes of Oklahoma

First U.S. edition May, 2026

Editor and Publisher   Laura LeHew

Proofreaders: TBD

Copyright © 2026   Uttered Chaos

All Rights Reserved. Except for brief passages quoted in a newspaper, magazine, radio or television review, no portion of this book may be reproduced in any form or by any means, electronic or mechanical, including photocopying and recording, or by any information storage and retrieval system, without written permission from the Publisher. All rights to the works printed herein remain with the author.

ISBN: 978-0-9998334-9-0

Uttered Chaos
391 Brae Burn Dr.
Eugene, OR 97405
www.utteredchaos.org
541-517-2198

These poems and photos are dedicated to anyone unable to fully enjoy the outdoors, travel comfortably, or maintain full mobility.

I want to acknowledge my family and friends who encouraged me to share my photography and poetry. Because of each of you, I have gained confidence in sharing through online platforms, art shows, spoken word, and other public events. Special thanks to Coreen for being the spark that ignited this project, and for her unwavering belief in my art.

Contents

River of Life

The river that we travel together
At times over treacherous rapids
Or under fierce conditions
We breathe deeply
Savoring the moments of
Welcome calm
However long, or brief
They strengthen us
For the rapids which inevitably appear again
Our hands clasping one another
Through those trying times
Which strain and separate us
One from the other
Sometimes they try violently
Sometimes insidiously

Then, like a soft wind
Gently snatching your hat away
Come those moments of calm, whether days or months
Becoming treasured memories
Gifts from the gods
Who bless our love
One for another
Our lives lived better
For the love shared
On the wild, wonderful, and unpredictable ride
Of the river of life.

I'm Still a Hottie

I'm still a hottie
      I think I wear my years well
My hotness may not be as obvious
      As years gone by
It only becomes apparent
      In flashes now
Dew on my brow
      Deodorant breaking down
Taking off as many clothes
      As convention and company will allow
Stepping outside into
      A bitter winter wind
Deeply grateful for the relief
      It provides
In my mature years
      When the heat rises
From deep within
      And is only assuaged
By the welcome
      Winter winds.

I Dreamed

Of a land filled with
A kind and warm people
Whose love for their land
and sea
For the bounty they provided
Was immense, along with their
Understanding of their
responsibility
As stewards of the land and water
Outsiders came
To pillage and rape
Both the land and her people
Their mutual suffering reverberated
Through lives and time
Devastating to the land
To those who loved her
Strengthened by their
Ancestors
Those who have gone before
They endured the atrocities
Upon themselves
Upon the land and waters
Entrusted to them
By the Creator
Until the sun rose, as always
Upon a new day of reckoning
When the beloved land
Was once again treated with
Kindness and love
By the descendants
Who love and respect
Who cherish her *still*

Their love renewing her
Just as she sustains all
Today's stewards of the earth
work to sustain her in return.

Invisible

This is how I feel
        He said
Holding up his napkin
        In front of his face
What?
        His date asked, startled
What do you mean?

I feel,
        He said
Invisible
        With you on your phone
While I'm sitting here
        Across the restaurant table
Since our agreement was
        No phones at the table
The agreement wasn't
        No conversation
No acknowledgement
        Of one another
It was
        No phones
It was
        Conversation
It was.

Twisted Childhood

The voices come first
        Loud…then louder
Through the walls
        Through the pillows
I hold tight
        Over my head
Both hands pressing
        Against my years
Suddenly there's banging
        As a body
Hits a wall
        The wall between us
Shakes from the impact
        Just as my breath
Shakes and my heart
        Races in fear
My belly clenches
        As my body begins to shake
In sync
        with the wall
Screams follow
        I pull the pillow tighter
Screams follow
        Tears flow
Inundating my pillow
        healing nothing.

Silence

I can't tell you
        What you mean
                To me
Because
        To do so
                Would create
Such vulnerability
        Requiring
                More courage
Than
        my heart
                contains

Gaslighting

What a weird term
            for something so twisted
She doesn't remember it
            that way
You misunderstood
            what I meant
You took it
            the wrong way
That's
            your story
That's her story and his story
            of abuse
Their story
            of abusers
Cleverly disguised
            as loved ones
Familiar clothing
            familiar faces
Gaslighting
            making her question
Their own
            sanity
Good grief.
            Why are they still there?

Your Bitter Heart

Your bitter heart
      Is showing through
The façade you show
      You know you do
That clever mask
      Which you wear
The mask of concern
      Of heartfelt care
We see through
      To the hatred within
No longer can you hide
      In the skin you're in
We were shocked
      And dismayed
When your mask
      Slipped and strayed
Exposing to us all
      The façade you'd made
So clever and conniving
      So well played
Your bitter heart
      Is so very clear
It's what you hold
      Near and dear.

Cracks

Cracks

There's a crack in our friendship
        I never saw before
Blissfully aware of the beautiful
        Solid entirety
Blinded to the subtle crack
        Growing inside
I saw only
        What I wanted to see
Love, concern, warmth
        And care
Not realizing jealousy was growing
        Between us
A tiny crack at first
        Growing day by day
Suddenly it was so obvious
        This glaring fissure
Of which I'd been blissfully
        Unaware
Nearly a year gone by
        My hindsight now 20/20
The words of others
        Protective of me
Now ring loudly
        True
I'm letting you go
        To be unhealthy somewhere else
Go be a backstabber
        A liar and a thief
In your own life
        Not in mine
I will winnow you away
        From the healthy people I love   ...

I will protect them
        From you
Only wishing I had seen that crack
        Years before.

Orange Rose

Orange Rose

Dedicated to Winona Marie Maupin Youngren

Dig it up
        I told my son
Put it in a pot
        And in my car

I drove it across the continent
        After she died
Once home
        I carried it lovingly inside

Placed it next to a large
        Window
Where it could be caressed
        By the sun

It's blossomed three times
        Since her last day
I like to think
        It's her

Echoing over and over
        Those many miles and nights
Since
        She passed away

Remembering
        Always
She heard my first breath
        I heard her last.

(Inspired by Crystal Shade)

Sorry, Not Sorry

The text appeared
   stark on my phone
The laughter burst forth
   from long un-kissed lips
Laughter fell and rolled
   and burst into garlands
In the air around me
   Falling in clouds of petals
Colorful and slowly descending
   around me
Healing as they fell
   Gently enveloping me
In color and soft care
   Sorry, not sorry
That you're single now…

INACTION
IS NOT
AN OPTION!

Fall 2020, Fall 2024, Fall 2026 ...

Your lies fall like autumn leaves
Scattering in the winds of a fall election
Your party sues to keep my neighbors from voting
Lines form around unnecessarily limited polling places
Hours on weary feet energized by steadfast hearts
Strangers bring water, food, chairs to share
Solidarity builds determined hearts
Voters will vote despite all obstacles
Honoring those women, and people of color
Whose fight to vote lives within us all
The trauma embedded in our DNA
They suffered so we could stand in line
Exercising our right to vote, to choose our leaders
To choose our laws, to stand against fascism
Against the tide of white supremacy, racism and fear
To speak out for justice
For our Black brothers and sisters
For all our relations from all walks of life
Unite!
Stand shoulder to shoulder
With me as we seek to save the future
Of the seventh generation
Of a tired planet
Of hopes and dreams we must realize
Uniting all nations
America, you were born on our land
Your birth spasms almost destroyed us
With your violent, unfettered greed
Now we stand, with hands extended
Hoping you'll reach out and grasp them
Focusing on being stewards of this land
And of the democracy we gave you.

He Said

Lay me down in the tall grass
Let me do my stuff
When your heart is hurting
And tears are not enough
To ease the ache in your body and heart
Lay back and let me drive
It's time to make a fresh start
Give yourself to me
Trust my love and my touch
Let me gentle both
I need you so much
Just lay back and let me drive
Feel the love between us begin to grow
Just believe and let yourself go
Let my love in
Let it flourish and show.

Too Much Truth

After so many lies
       covering the floor
Crawling up the walls
       creeping across the ceiling
Spilling out onto the
       wet, slippery sidewalk
Sliding up and over
       the unsuspecting car
Slithering into the minute
       openings into the engine
Covering up the seats
       slipping into the trunk
Sliding down the long,
       long, steep driveway
Infiltrating bodies
       and unsuspecting hearts
Filling every nook and cranny
       of our lives
'Til all life and love
       is left choking
Gasping for one last,
       lonely breath

California Girl

Sitting in my truck
       next to my man
I see you avoiding
       my eyes
When did your illicit relationship
       begin?
Are you why he pushed me
       away?
That cold, lonely
       summer night
Was he already pretending
       to be faithful to you?
While being utterly faithless
       to me?

Run

Run

Run, girl run!
If he'll cheat on his wife…

Promises sworn before
The Creator

On a warm summer day
Before loved ones

Then you cannot expect
Anything else

Take it from me,
Wait… you already did.

Changes

Freezing rain on the windows
Holding the dark of night at bay
Relieved by the not-so-gentle white
Beginning to blanket the welcoming earth
From stubby shrubs
To towering trees so tall
They touch the sky
Leftover leaves letting go
To grieve the passing
Of the season
Where beauty abounded
Where a sparkling beauty now
Begins.

Love

Love

We sing about it
          Pray for it
          Imagine what it may be like
          Hope for a healthy relationship
Talk endlessly to
          Our friends
          And family
          About it
How it shapes our lives
          Our activities
          Our hopes and our dreams
How it can
          Shatter
          Everything
Yeah, we yearn
          for it
          and so much more.

I Write

I Write

Because I can
        because others cannot
Their voices silenced
        forever
By gatling guns
        by boarding schools
By racism, violence
        rape, genocide and greed
My ancestors
        use my voice
I welcome them
        to speak through me
To tell their stories
        from tragedy to triumph
To speak for those
        Silenced by time
        By culture
        By cruelty
I speak
I speak
I speak
I speak.

Burn For Me

Give me a little bite
        He said, playfully
Referring to my poetry
        Insinuating it has no bite
But I do
        Oh, yes, I do
Prepare yourself
        Do you have the strength?
To take my bite
        Warm and sharp…
A nip
        Followed by a tongue
Tempt me not
        You know not what you seek
Don't start a fire
        You can't put out.

No White Foods

No white foods
	Sweet Medicine told us
Long before
	The White man came
With lard
	To clog your arteries
Sugar
	To make us diabetic
Flour
	To pack on the pounds
Milk
	To give us extra hormones
Salt
	To give us kidney stones
No white foods
	Our prophet said
Knowing before he should
	That they would kill us
After the bullets
	Stopped flying
After the howitzers stilled
	And the smoke blew away
After the screaming
	And the bleeding ended
After we were
	Invited at gunpoint
To live on reservations
	Concentration camps
Before they were
	Called that
Now we eat
	Lard, sugar, salt, flour, drink milk
Forgetting the words
	Of wisdom
                                        ...

Handed down
        To us
Generation to generation
        One after another
Our oral tradition
        Serving us well
But some choose to
        Ignore the wisdom
Of those who went
        Before
Choosing instead
        Convenience
Comfort over
        Health
Cheap over
        Traditional gathering
Yet
        Some gather
And hunt
        Still
I see roots
        Drying in a window
Gathered with song
        With care
With hope
        And tradition.

Sunshine

Sunshine

Warms my arms, my face
       Exposed to the healing rays
My mind drifts away
       On the fluffy clouds above me
Warmed by the sun
       Protected from the gentle autumn breeze
I relax
       I let go. I let go…
Gravity holds me
       To the earth
To this enveloping
       Buffalo robe beneath me
To the grass and earth
       Beneath the robe
To the spinning planet
       Of my ancestors
As well as of yours
       I feel the spin
In my mind
       And heart
I am one with the earth
       I am no one without the earth.

Healing

Healing

The words tumble from our lips
        Into our phones
        Onto paper
        Into a microphone

We share them over tea
        Coffee
        During a long walk or
        A late night call

Our stories fall from our lips
        Into the ears
        Of those we trust
        Where they're safe, protected

The healing begins
        With the sharing
        Of our pain
        Of our trauma
        Sharing with receptive, caring audiences

Our healing, as women
        And as men
        Lies in having someone to trust
        Someone to listen and advise

Our healing lies in the
        Unburdening of our hearts
        And the sharing of trust
        Along with the advice which follows

Our healing is
        Every honest conversation
        Following
        "How are you?"

Choices That You Make

Choices That You Make

There's hatred in your face
While your lips are dripping lies
There is no surprise or shock
Watching you unravel our family ties

The love that held us together
That carried us so long
Once helped us all
Now it's all twisted and wrong

You don't like to drink beer
It's not your drug of choice
You prefer coke or meth
They help you find your voice

I lecture until I'm blue in the face
It gives you a temper you never had before
Makes us afraid of you
But makes you just want more

Drugs are tearing up our lives
Once full of laughter and love
Now so torn by the aftereffects of your choices
A shadow of the family we dreamed of

We're in a war zone now
All captives of your crime
All praying for the day
When it's rehab time.

Nature's Fury

Nature's Fury

The wind raged as the waves pounded the shore
      Competing against one another
      To see which could do the most damage
Sweeping huge logs ashore
      As if they were the cast off toys of giant children
      Bored and destructive
Each wave grasping deeply into the sand
      Drawing away the beauty
      That once was
When the sun rises tomorrow
      And caresses the earth
      On a new landscape
The battered beach will prevail
      Her strength and continuity a testimony
      The stunning silence that follows
The bitter storm
      Bringing peace and joy
      As the breeze, soft and gentle
Making up for its previous frenzy
      Caresses each low wave
      Subdued after the storm.

Racism

I'm here to tell you now
       How sick I am of hearing
From unwitting, ethnocentric
       Ignoramuses
That racism doesn't exist
       Anymore
Please tell that to the families
       Of Tamir Rice
       Sandra Bland
       Breonna Taylor
       Trayvon Martin
Or any of the five dead Black people
Shot down while walking near their Tulsa, Oklahoma homes

Guilty, guilty, guilty
       Of the capital crime – NBW
Not Being White
Tell that to the blind Native man
Hospitalized with great need of heart surgery
Held for days
       Prepped day after day
       Until, finally he is cut open
Operated on
Then while in recovery
       Sneered at for requesting pain medicine
By those who have sworn
       To "first do no harm"
Denigrated for NBW-Not Being White
Carved into his chest
Initials, "KKK"
       An obscene autograph
Left by some racist f'ing educated idiot
Marking his territory
       In the operating room   ...

Forever scarred this blind Native elder
Who thankfully could not see
The graffiti embedded forever
        In his skin. On his body.
Forever on his skin
Tell my son, there is no racism
        After his Mom
        Was assaulted in front of him
        By White people
While peacefully protesting
        Against intolerance
Tell my heart, my community
        My country, my continent
There is no racism
        While we have to beg
For jurisdiction over those who assault
        Our women and children
        Ourselves. Myself.
One out of every four
        We informed the UN
        We begged for protection
        For the right
To prosecute those
        Who see us as
        Vulnerable
                As victims
                To their war crimes
War against those daring to live while
        Not Being White
I only know one Native woman who hasn't
        Been assaulted
I don't know a Native man who hasn't
Been assaulted for
        Not Being White   ...

The next time you think
    Racism doesn't exist anymore
Think on my words
    On my experiences
    On the experiences of too many people
    Too many human beings
Guilty. Guilty. Guilty.
    Of Not Being White.

I Am the Chipmunk

Running free, scrambling
    Nimbly up a tree
My steps quick and sure
    My heart is clean and pure
Focused am I, on the inevitable
    Upcoming winter
Food is my focus
    It drives my life
As I deftly dance
    between ever smaller limbs
Navigating my barked highway
    Under a clear blue sky
Work while weather is good
    Pack my food away
Learn from my elders
    The wisdom of planning
Sharing my knowledge, unknowingly
    With the two-legged beneath my tree.

Web of Life

It's a web Grandmother Spider has
        Woven all around us
Some imagine themselves self-supporting
        Isolated and alone
Not realizing how intimately their life
        Affects others
A casual greeting at the grocery store
        To a cashier having a bad day
A door held by a young man after he
        Ran to get there before a woman could open it herself
With the words,
        "My Mom raised me right."
        Followed by a bright smile
A warm hug for a friend
        Seen too infrequently
The moment cherished by the heart as well as
        By the body
Simple strands of simple lives shared in
        Moments of connection
Lives enriched by the web connecting us all
        In one way or another
A web that enriches while it creates
        Unwitting connections.

Choose Your Path

inspired by Kunu Bearchum-hochunk, Northern Cheyenne

Walk in the path of our ancestors
      your feet leaving only the faintest of footprints
Walk the Red Road
      with purpose and intent
Always remembering how important it is
      to be a good ancestor

We stand in the lands
      of our ancestors
We grow our crops
      and our children
In the lands of our ancestors
      where their bones still lie
Except for those stolen
      for museums and gawkers
From bygone days
      when we weren't considered human

We stand united with other
      water protectors
We are land, air, fishing, hunting and treaty
      protectors and stewards
Like our ancestors before us
      fought to be and do
Everyone trying to preserve
      and protect our people
Our lands
      our very way of life

We stand while we build
      our gardens, our business, our communities
We are uniting in language
      protection, preservation and promotion
Our languages hold
         ...

culture, history, philosophy
They teach lessons
        through storytelling, oral history
Our people, our resilience
        our strength together and alone

We stand for human rights
        not just our own
We are the caretakers
        of Turtle Island
Our people are
        our strength and our future
The laughter of children
        once stolen from our communities
Now thrive and grow
        like the lush plants in our gardens

We grow food
        harvesting what we've planted
We are growing ourselves
        where we've been planted
Our nations
        growing through love and creativity
Sending our children
        to college, to learn and grow their minds
We aren't perfect
        we're only trying to be human

Walk in the path of our ancestors
        your feet leaving only the faintest of footprints
Walk the Red Road
        with purpose and intent
Always remembering how important it is
        to be a good ancestor

Né-Méhotatse

Né-Méhotatse

Means
> I love you

Means
> I care about you

Means
> I want life
> To treat you kindly

Means
> I want a healthy life
> For you

Means
> I want to be there
> If, and when you need me

Means
> I will speak true
> To you, even if it's hard

Means
> I won't stand idly by
> If addiction tries to steal you from me

Means
> I believe in tough love

Means
> I love you.

Remember When

When I was young
        I was nearly invincible
        my strength had no limits I could discern
Sports were fun and easy
        my energy was immense
        downhill skiing in the mornings, water skiing in the
afternoons
Running was my refuge
        miles fell behind me
        the wind lifted my feet, pushing my back and myself
Pushing myself to run
        further and faster
        to help me focus on what I could do
When I wrote
        my words were for myself
        my internal pain bled through my pen onto pages and pages
            lost to time

When I went away to college
        I left the pain behind
        decades before "no contact" was a catch phrase
When I was there, I ran
        track and cross country and convinced to join the cross
country skiing team
        although I didn't know how to ski, humbled by crashing into
small, snow covered trees
Two years later
        burnt out by competing in 2-3 college sports
        and working 2-3 part time jobs, which took their toll
I left college for love
        and to restart my life, as I knew it
        reinventing myself and relocating to the lands of the Hawaiian
            nation   ...

When I wrote
>my words filled pages painted by my typewriter
>typing other's papers for money or food

When I married
>after dating for nearly five years
>I chose a taker
Whose insatiable hunger for our resources
>and other women
>led to an unexpected freedom
I had naively thought
>that vows had meaning
>promises were meant to be kept
When I was suddenly single, it was a relief
>seeing the end coming
>years before it arrived
When I wrote
>It was of the pain, inexplicable
>inexorable and unavoidable

When I raised my children
>alone, but not alone
>family uplifting us all
There were struggles
>nights lit by candles, not electricity
>jobs taken for need, not for a ladder
When I wrote
>it was sparingly, words barely flowing
>from a heart torn asunder, sewn back together by little hands
>>and hearts
>>>>...

When I went back to college
          suddenly forty and still single after several years
          bolstered by a dream, hope and prayers
Studying night and day
          working odd jobs to support
          my college dream, my family and myself
Focused on my children and myself
          while planning intently for the future
When I walked
          in my regalia
          my beaded grad cap worn with pride on that bright, sunny day

My dream
          for a degree, now fired up for another,
          inspired by those who have gone before me
Inspired by professors
          who meant well and saw in me
          more than I saw in myself
I studied
          night and day
          living by my schedule and fueled by my dreams
Laser focused,
          all my assignments listed
          for each consecutive term, zealously
When I wrote
          it was of the land and our history
          the history of my people

When I worked out
          it was to release the stress, the strain
          of all within me   ...

My body stronger
        almost, than my mind
        which carried me through grad school
The gym was my refuge
        the Native American Longhouse and all who sought refuge
            there
        became family
Years had passed
        typewriters and word processors had fallen
                for computers and flash drives
When I wrote
        it was for my courses and the college paper
        which rattled those who didn't want to read about minorities

When I realized I wasn't young
        my bones grinding against one another
        injuries demanding their due respect
I realized, after referring to someone as, "that kid"
        when they were in their 30's
        using "thank you, dear" far more frequently than I'd ever
            done
My mind suddenly full
        of memories, experiences, education
        layered with ceremony, song and dances

Suddenly all those years
        were filled with road trips to Oklahoma
        South Dakota, pow wows, sweats, ceremonies
When I wrote
        it was infused with culture
        colored by resistance, by resilience and uplifted by prayer   ...

When I realized
        why old people wear comfy clothing
        and wide, goofy shoes
I realized that I, too
        was now an elder
        in comfy clothes and wide shoes
That my former fashionista self
        had traded high heels for hiking boots
        miniskirts for below the knee ribbon skirts
Red dust covered bare skin
        at Colony pow wow
        where I danced for my father, whose flag was flown in his
            honor
When I wrote
        my words were passionate
        inviting in the voices of those who have gone before

When I die
        my words will end with me
        carried within my spirit to the next world
There will be words
        on the leaves of the White man
        left behind, forgotten and unnecessary
Words that once may have seemed
        so important, needful of their own space
        will be left behind
In books, magazines,
        forgotten legal pads and random scraps of paper
        holding unsung songs, poems that will never be read
When I wrote it was for my people and to release my own pain
        to tell stories filled with culture and laughter
            I hope others remember that writing was my refuge, my
            release, my way of life.

Back Row Poet Society

There they are all in a row
       hidden, they mistakenly think
No one can hear or see them
       until one's whispered aside
Ripples down the row
       laughter grows exponentially
As the joke is told, louder and louder
       struggling to be heard over uncontrollable laughter
Bursting forth from compressed lips
       out of well-fed bellies
Now shaking unrestrained
       and unashamed
The gales of laughter rise
       and spread throughout the room
Drowning out the clatter of forks
       the sounds of clinking glasses
The joke travels quickly
       almost faster than a smile
The laughter rises like a warm wind
       Floating to the sturdy rafters above
Falling back gently into welcoming smiles
       knowing looks shared across the room
Oh, those back row poets
       you can't take them anywhere!

Three Words:
For • Love • Village

For the love of my village
   I stand
For the love of my people
   My spine is firm
For the love of others in my village
   My hand is outstretched
For those who need music
   I sing
For those who don't have the ability
   I dance
For the love of my village
   I am.

She Doesn't Know

Dedicated to Lauri Langston

We do, though
She doesn't know
How much she is loved
She doesn't notice
How we flock around her
      Fluttering for her attention
She thinks
We are just being kind
She doesn't see who we see
The beauty and kindness
Which radiates from her
      A cascade of mountain water pouring over us
Her laughter is infectious
Her glances, knowing and inferring
Causing us to laugh as well
Just from her silly glances
Her bawdy jokes
      Giving us gales of laughter
Her story
Is not mine to tell
But she shares glimpses
Stories that carry lessons
For us to learn from
      Teaching through oral history
She doesn't know
How much we love her
So, we tell her again, and again
Reminding her that she is needed.
Reminding her that she is loved.
      Reminders she gives to everyone around her.

www.ingramcontent.com/pod-product-compliance
Lightning Source LLC
Chambersburg PA
CBHW072048150726
47996CB00015B/2102